Italians in Michigan

DISCOVERING THE PEOPLES OF MICHIGAN
Arthur W. Helweg and Linwood H. Cousins, Series Editors

Ethnicity in Michigan: Issues and People
Jack Glazier, Arthur W. Helweg

French Canadians in Michigan
John P. DuLong

African Americans in Michigan
Lewis Walker, Benjamin C. Wilson, Linwood H. Cousins

Albanians in Michigan
Frances Trix

Jews in Michigan
Judith Levin Cantor

Amish in Michigan
Gertrude Enders Huntington

Italians in Michigan
Russell M. Magnaghi

Discovering the Peoples of Michigan is a series of publications examining the state's rich multicultural heritage. The series makes available an interesting, affordable, and varied collection of books that enables students and lay readers to explore Michigan's ethnic dynamics. A knowledge of the state's rapidly changing multicultural history has far-reaching implications for human relations, education, public policy, and planning. We believe that Discovering the Peoples of Michigan will enhance understanding of the unique contributions that diverse and often unrecognized communities have made to Michigan's history and culture.

Italians in Michigan

Russell M. Magnaghi

Michigan State University Press

East Lansing

⊗ The paper used in this publication meets the minimum requirements
of ANSI/NISO Z39.48-1992 (R 1997) (Permanence of Paper)

Michigan State University Press
East Lansing, Michigan 48823-5202
Printed and bound in the United States of America

07 06 05 04 03 02 01   1 2 3 4 5 6 7

LIBRARY OF CONGRESS CATALOGING-IN-PUBLICATION DATA
Magnaghi, Russell M.
Italians in Michigan / Russell M. Magnaghi.
p. cm. — (Discovering the peoples of Michigan)
Includes bibliographical references and index.
ISBN 0-87013-599-6 (pbk. : alk. paper)
1. Italian Americans—Michigan—History. 2. Italian Americans—Michigan—
Social conditions. 3. Immigrants—Michigan—History. 4. Michigan—
Ethnic relations. 5. Michigan—Social conditions. I. Title. II. Series.
F575.I8 M34 2001
305.8510774—dc21
2001003456

Discovering the Peoples of Michigan. The editors wish
to thank the Kellogg Foundation for their generous support.

Cover design by Ariana Grabec-Dingman
Book design by Sharp Des!gns, Inc.

COVER PHOTO: Italian dramatic group, Negaunee,
Michigan, 1928. Dominic & Joyce Chiri Collection.

Visit Michigan State University Press on the World Wide Web at:
www.msupress.msu.edu

This book is dedicated to
Leonard Altobello
and
Monsignor David Spelgatti

SERIES ACKNOWLEDGMENTS

Discovering the Peoples of Michigan is a series of publications that resulted from the cooperation and effort of many individuals. The people recognized here are not a complete representation, for the list of contributors is too numerous to mention. However, credit must be given to Jeffrey Bonevich, who worked tirelessly with me on contacting people as well as researching and organizing material.

The initial idea for this project came from Mary Erwin, but I must thank Fred Bohm, director of the Michigan State University Press, for seeing the need for this project, for giving it his strong support, and for making publication possible. Also, the tireless efforts of Keith Widder and Elizabeth Demers, senior editors at Michigan State University Press were vital in bringing DPOM to fruition. Keith put his heart and soul into this series, and his dedication was instrumental in its success.

Otto Feinstein and Germaine Strobel of the Michigan Ethnic Heritage Studies Center patiently and willingly provided names for contributors and constantly gave this project their tireless support.

My late wife, Usha Mehta Helweg, was the initial editor. She meticulously went over manuscripts. Her suggestions and advice were crucial. Initial typing, editing, and formatting were also done by Majda Seuss, Priya Helweg, and Carol Nickolai.

Many of the maps in the series were drawn by Fritz Seegers while the graphics showing ethnic residential patterns in Michigan were done by the Geographical Information Center (GIS) at Western Michigan University under the directorship of David Dickason. Additional maps have been contributed by Ellen White.

Russell Magnaghi must also be given special recognition for his willingness to do much more than be a contributor. He provided author contacts as well as information to the series' writers. Other authors and organizations provided comments on other aspects of the work. There are many people that were interviewed by the various authors who will remain anonymous. However, they have enabled the story of their group to be told. Unfortunately, their names are not available, but we are grateful for their cooperation.

Most of all, this work is a tribute to the writers who patiently gave their time to write and share their research findings. Their contributions are noted and appreciated. To them goes most of the gratitude.

ARTHUR W. HELWEG, *Series Co-editor*

Contents

Italians in Michigan

For over 350 years Italian immigrants have played an important role in the opening and development of Michigan. The first immigrants came with the French in the seventeenth century. A second migration took place between 1840 and 1880, as a small but growing number of Italian laborers were attracted to the state's northern mining regions. The third era, the traditional period of massive immigration, began in the 1880s and lasted until 1924. Finally, a few immigrants from Italy came to Michigan after World War II.

The story of Italian migration to Michigan is divided between Lower and Upper Peninsula experiences, which produced a dichotomy: Italians, usually attracted to urban-industrial centers, first migrated to the rural and remote Upper Peninsula. Of the 3,088 Italians in Michigan in 1890, 2,386 (77.3%) resided in the Upper Peninsula while only 702 (22.7%) lived in the Lower Peninsula. The copper and iron mining counties were home to the vast majority of the Italians: 2,277 (74%) while only 379 (12.2%) made their homes in Detroit and Wayne County. Between 1890 and 1930 the Italian population dramatically shifted from the Upper to the Lower Peninsula, stimulated by labor unrest and the developing automobile industry. In 1930, out of 43,087 Italians in the state, 73% resided in Wayne County and only 11% in the mining counties. Thus, this study will be divided between the two Peninsulas.

The family was the most central and important institution in the lives of Italians, and it had its effect on them in the Michigan experience. The family is an essential factor in explaining individual motives and social mechanisms for departure from the Old Country and subsequent adjustment to American life. Although unattended men comprised the bulk of the earliest immigrants they were soon followed by wives and children, a situation that aided demographic and community growth throughout Michigan.

First Immigration

During the French regime, Italy did not exist as a nation but rather as a geographical expression. For centuries the French, Spanish, and Austrians dominated the Italian peninsula. As a result, Italians who sought opportunity in the New World traveled to France and came to North America under the French flag.

A number of Italians in Michigan's colonial past came as administrators, chroniclers, explorers, fur traders, and soldiers. The only Italian Jesuit missionary to serve in New France was the Roman, Francesco G. Bressani, S. J. (1626-1672), who ministered to the Huron Indians in Canada. Although he never traveled as far as Michigan, in 1653 he wrote of the Ojibwa of Sault Ste. Marie and described the Upper Peninsula.

The Tonty, or Tonti, brothers, Enrico (1649/50-1704) and Alfonso (c. 1659-1727), were directly connected to Michigan. After an unsuccessful revolt against their Spanish overlords, the Tonti family fled to France where the sons achieved success. Enrico arrived as a lieutenant of René-Robert Cavelier de La Salle in 1679. He supervised the construction of the *Griffon*, the first sailing vessel in the Great Lakes. Tonti passed through Michigan on numerous occasions, traveling to the Illinois Country. Having achieved rank as one of the major explorers and fur traders of North America, he succumbed to yellow fever in Mobile in 1704.[1]

His brother, Alfonso, proved to be a successful fur trader and a worrisome administrator. He arrived in New France in 1685 and a dozen years later was appointed commandant at Fort Buade on the north side of the Straits of Mackinac, becoming wealthy from the fur trade. When Cadillac established Detroit in July 1701, Alfonso was his second in command. Although an able leader, his considerable involvement in trading ventures caused the Crown to remove Tonti in 1705. After serving in several outposts, in 1717 he again assumed command of Detroit and quickly reverted to his old habits. Although the *habitants* at Detroit disliked him, Tonti was a friend of the governor and remained in office until his death.[2]

As was true with the Tonti brothers and other Italians, their names became frenchified; thus, it becomes difficult to identify their Italian origin. The Florentine priest, Constantine Del Halle, whose Italian name was Degli Agli, exemplifies this process. He arrived at Detroit in July 1702 and served as pastor of Ste. Anne's church until his accidental death in 1706. A number of other Italian fur traders and farmers also settled the frontier, such as Joseph Andrew *dit* l'Italien from Milan.[3]

In the summer of 1791 Count Paolo Andreani visited the Lake Superior Country, leading a scientific expedition to study the shape of the earth. He is considered the first known European to make a continuous circumnavigation of Lake Superior.[4]

Numerous Italians worked in Michigan during the first half of the nineteenth century. Father Samuel Mazzuchelli (1806-1864), a Dominican priest from Milan, served Ste. Anne's parish on Mackinac Island during the early 1830s. Another Milanese priest, Father Toussaint Santelli, also ministered at Mackinac between 1838 and 1843. Even though he profited from his involvement in the fur trade, the harsh climate forced him to relocate to Monroe, Michigan, for a few months before he returned to Milan in 1844.[5] In the 1830s and 1840s, some transient Italian traders operated out of Mackinac Island. The Trabbic brothers, Peter (1822-1903) and John (1823-1916), from Liguria, settled in Erie Township around 1836. They eventually owned over a thousand acres of land in Erie and married locally. Their descendants continue to live in the area.[6]

Between 1860 and 1880, as Michigan emerged as a destination for Italian immigrants, Italy went through unification and national development. Poor economic and social conditions in Italy, including limited land ownership, long hours, poor wages, unscrupulous land

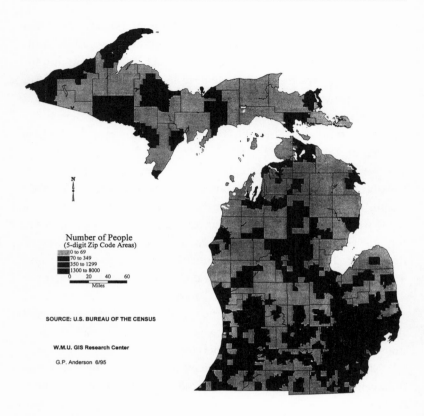

Number of People
(5-digit Zip Code Areas)
0 to 69
70 to 349
350 to 1299
1300 to 8000
0   20   40   60
Miles

SOURCE: U.S. BUREAU OF THE CENSUS

W.M.U. GIS Research Center

G.P. Anderson 6/95

Figure 1. Distribution of Michigan's Population Claiming Italian Ancestry.

owners, and high taxes sent thousands of young immigrants to the New World. America offered dramatic opportunities for economic and social improvements. In the mid-nineteenth century Michigan's cities and mining centers stood on the brink of economic expansion, needing labor to fuel their growth.

The Lower Peninsula

Detroit and Detroit Area

Bustling Detroit began to attract individual Italians beginning in the mid-nineteenth century. Some of the earliest immigrants were Italian sailors who had sailed the Great Lakes. Angelo Paldi moved to Detroit in the early 1840s as a bandmaster with the 5th U.S. Infantry, and remained in Michigan after his discharge in 1848. Other Italians, like Dr. Luigi Cavalli, settled in Detroit and developed their own businesses. Cavalli opened an 8,000-item natural history museum that his heirs sold to the Smithsonian Institution after his death in 1853. By 1855 Swiss-Italians, Genoese, Tuscans, and Neapolitans who operated small businesses and boarding houses comprised the Italian community of Detroit.[7] Four years later Italian organ grinders and vendors worked selling plaster statues on the streets.[8] This type of migration by a few Italian entrepreneurs was common in the mid-nineteenth century.

The sons of many of these early Italian settlers served in the Civil War. The career of Angelo Paldi Jr. is indicative of immigrant service in the Union Army. Although forty-five years of age, he joined the 1st Michigan Cavalry at Pontiac with the rank of captain and was soon promoted to major. He was wounded at Brandy Station, Virginia, in October 1863, and again at the Battle of the Wilderness on 6 May 1864. After he was discharged from the Army he returned to his farm in Brockway.[9]

After 1855 Italian immigration increased through the intervention of Vital Forni, a Swiss-Italian. Soon Nicholas and Angela Lagorio, Stefano Garbarino, and the Schiappacasse family from Liguria migrated to Detroit. In 1880 a group of Lombards who were headed for Calumet were intercepted by local Italians and encouraged to remain in Detroit. A year later the Lagorios aided a second group of Lombards, who, in turn, started chain migration from their hometown of Cuggiono, west of Milan. Sicilians from Terrasina and Trapini arrived in 1875. During bad economic times in 1883 other Sicilian families, who were in the fruit business, migrated from Cleveland to Detroit.[10] A stable Italian colony evolved and according to a special church census taken in 1897, there were 1,733 Italians living in the Detroit area. In the coming decades Italians came from every region in Italy including some from the Republic of San Marino, and in the twentieth century, a small member of Venetian Jews.[11]

By 1900 many Italians found jobs in Detroit's growing manufacturing industries, while many others contributed to an expanding service

Figure 2. Italian workers on the Ford Model A assembly line, Rouge Plant, Dearborn, Michigan, 8 March 1928. Photo ID: P.833.51076, from the collections of Henry Ford Museum & Greenfield Village.

economy. The Genoese and Sicilians vended fruit, while most Lombards labored in foundries and factories. The Neapolitans constructed streets and railroads. The Venetians and Tuscans used their skills with stucco, terrazzo, and mosaic to help build the Detroit post office and the Wayne County Building. Others owned groceries and barrooms, made shoes, or worked as tailors at department stores.

The immigrants were intent on making Detroit their permanent home. Although Italian laborers made $1.50 per ten-hour day, they saved and invested in small homes. By 1901 the Detroit Italians owned $400,000 in urban property.[12]

According to the 1900 federal census 905 Italians lived in Detroit, but this number grew dramatically as Detroit and other communities in southern Michigan expanded with the booming automobile industry. Within the decade there were 5,724 Italians in Detroit alone. Henry Ford's astounding offer of $5.00 per day stimulated further revision. In

1915 some 683 Italians worked among 13,000 foreign-born workers employed by the Ford Motor Company. In 1920, 16,205 Italians lived in Detroit. This number grew to 28,581 in 1930. There were also 979 Italians in neighboring Highland Park and 277 in Hamtramck, many of whom found jobs at the local Ford and Chevrolet facilities and associated industries.

The cities located Downriver from Detroit also attracted many immigrants. Italians working at Ford's Rouge River facility lived in Dearborn or in the Downriver communities of River Rouge, Ecorse, Lincoln Park, and Trenton.[13] In Wyandotte, Italians, many of them Sicilians, found employment at Great Lakes Steel, J. B. Ford (the alkali industry), Michigan Alkali Plants, Detroit Soda Products, Pennsylvania Salt, and All-Metal Products.

In Detroit, for many years, the shops, halls, and churches of "Little Italy" existed along Gratiot Avenue and its side streets. As Italians moved northward, Sicilians developed another Italian community called *Cacalupo*[14] in the vicinity of Gratiot and Harper, close to the

Figure 3. Gratiot Avenue at McDougall looking north in the heart of Detroit's Little Italy, 20 April 1930. The Detroit News *Collection, Walter P. Reuther Library, Wayne State University.*

streetcar turn-around and terminal. By 2000 Italian Americans are concentrated in Wayne, Macomb, and Oakland counties, having moved northeast into the suburban communities of the Grosse Pointes and into Sterling Heights, Warren, Clinton Township, and New Baltimore.

Since the largest concentration of Italian immigrants was located in the Detroit area, many Italian-owned enterprises arose to meet the needs of their countrymen and women. There were so many businesses that they can be categorized into a number of specialties. The food service industry employed many Italians. One of the earliest Italians in this field was Luigi Schiappacasse, who came to the United States in 1865. He developed produce stands throughout the city and provided newly arrived immigrants with instant vending jobs. Eventually he expanded his business into wholesaling, and when he died in 1916 he was reputed to be one of the largest wholesale fruit merchants in Detroit.[15] Italian produce vendors sold their wares throughout the city. They progressed from stands to hand carts to horse-drawn wagons, and finally to trucks. Some of them became members of the Detroit Fruit Vendors Association. Many of these Italians opened retail and wholesale shops in the Eastern Market. Faro Vitale, "the watermelon king," sold melons from a pile in the back of an enormous truck. Today his son continues the tradition, selling hundreds of truckloads of watermelons each season. Other Italian American produce dealers still working out of the Eastern Market include: Charlie Palazzolo & Sons, Mercurio Brothers, Inc., Del Bene Produce, Ciaramitaro Brothers Produce, Rocky's Peanuts, and Tom Maceri & Sons.[16] On a different but related note, one of the first Italian florists in the Detroit area was Frank Loverde, who established his shop in 1921. Eventually he went on to become one of the largest flower wholesalers in the Detroit Metro region.

The grocery, bakery, and fruit market are three businesses closely associated with Italians. Located throughout the community, the groceries sell Italian cheeses, olives in brine, dried codfish, sausages, and imported olive oil. Today in Detroit's East Side there are over seventeen Italian bakeries offering a variety of ethnic pastries.[17] Dozens of produce markets found throughout the East Side provide a wide variety of fresh fruits and vegetables, meat, and breads.

Figure 4. Women weighing produce on a scale, Eastern Market, 1917. The Detroit News *Collection, Walter P. Reuther Library, Wayne State University.*

Some businesses grew into well-known local institutions, but did not survive. In 1914 Tuscan-born Alfredo Grilli established the once-flourishing Grilli Beverages, now closed. Roman Cleanser, a well-known cleaning powder in Detroit, has gone the way of Grilli's. Two products that continue to this day are Better Made Potato Chips, established by Peter Cipriano, and Alinosi Ice Cream.

The Italian restaurant exists throughout the state, ranging from simple pizzerias to sophisticated establishments specializing in regional dishes. A focal point for businessmen, merchants, and politicians is the Roma Cafe, the oldest Italian restaurant in Detroit, dating back to around 1889. The original café, operated by the Sossi family, is a popular eatery.

The production of floor tile, mosaic tile, and terrazzo flooring became important businesses in Detroit. A majority of the tile artisans came from San Marino. Many public and private buildings show the skills of these Italian artisans. Unfortunately, as the cost for such work is prohibitive, it is no longer done.

The Calcaterra and Bagnasco names have been attached to funeral homes in Detroit since 1908 and 1915 respectively. In the fall of 2000 the two businesses merged as a single entity.

Prior to the Depression, Vincenzo Giuliano, the publisher of the *Italian Tribune*, still in business, opened the Bank of Italy. As well, the Giuliano Travel Agency was a profitable enterprise because of the number of Italians who frequently traveled to the Old Country.

Among the early Italian immigrants a growing professional class emerged to serve the public. Physicians and dentists practiced within the community, and in 1914 George T. Cimini opened "La Farmacia Italiana." In the same year Dr. Frank C. Pacific opened his establishment as Detroit's first Italian optometrist.

Architect Louis Rosetti came from Italy in 1922. The firm of Giffels and Rosetti designed many of the city's civic center buildings, Grosse Pointe Yacht Club, Everett School, Cobo Hall, and Detroit Metro Airport. Italian Americans entered higher education, and by the first quarter of the twentieth century many of them had become attorneys, clergymen, dentists, engineers, pharmacists, physicians, teachers, and writers.[18]

Italians formed organizations to promote business. In 1919 the Italian vice consul, Pietro Cardiello, felt that the time was right to organize an Italian Chamber of Commerce. Several hundred businessmen rapidly joined its ranks. It played a prominent role in promoting Americanization among the immigrants and continues to promote local businesses and maintain commercial ties with Italy.

Italians in the Detroit Metro area took part in the labor movement. On 1 May 1909, the Italian socialists celebrated "*festa del lavoro*" or labor day.[19] Many joined the struggling ranks of organized labor. During the 1930s Osvaldo DeSpirt refused to scab and remained out of work for nearly four years in solidarity with the new terrazzo and tile workers union. Later, at the end of the decade, as unions were able to organize, many Italians joined them and worked into union leadership positions. Between 30 December 1936 and 11 February 1937, many Italians and Italian Americans participated in the strike against General Motors in Flint, the first large-scale sitdown strike in Michigan. In the mid-twentieth century the American Italian Labor Council, composed of independent and craft union leaders, was active in Detroit. Labor leaders

Nick DiGaetano, Joseph Basso, and Joseph F. Pagano have deposited their papers in the Walter Reuther Labor Archives at Wayne State University.

Traditionally women remained in the home where they nourished and maintained the family.[20] Many of them took in boarders or lodgers who provided the family with additional revenue. For example in Detroit in the spring of 1920, Jennie Dottore, whose husband Louis worked in an auto plant, took care of her son, her nephew, and six lodgers, who also worked in an auto plant. Virginia Saratoni, a widow, took four Italian lodgers into her home.[21] Some women sold home-made wine to make extra money.

Other Italian women found employment outside of the home. This was especially true of widows. Women like Agatha Bommarito managed a grocery store while her husband, Joe, worked in an auto factory. Pauline Cassanita worked as a cigar maker for her husband. Others found employment as waitresses. Italian American women broke with tradition and worked at a variety of jobs. Fifteen-year old Rose Christoferi sold confectionery in a candy store, Christina Marino installed electrical systems on cars, and Mary Grilli clerked in a bookstore.

Italian American women also joined the professional ranks. In 1918 Grace Bommarito became the first female Detroit-Italian pharmacist. Shortly after World War I, Rose Esperti became the first Italian female to study law in Detroit.[22]

Some Italian women rebelled against their husbands' wishes and decided either to establish or join Italian women's clubs or male club auxiliaries. In April 1956 Maria Giuliano and Maria Lalli founded the American Italian Professional and Business Women's Club. By the mid-twentieth century Italian women's organizations existed throughout Michigan.

Mutual beneficial lodges or societies were common in the Old Country, and they became popular in Italian communities throughout Michigan as well. For a monthly fee of fifty cents or more, these societies provided accident, health, and death benefits to their members. These organizations also offered the immigrant a place to socialize and celebrate Italian and American holidays with parades, speeches, lunches, dinners, and dances.[23] Many of these clubs restricted membership to individuals who came from a particular province or even town.[24]

The first club for men in Michigan was founded on 20 April 1873 as the Society of Italian Union and Brotherhood of Detroit. A host of other locals started over the years. In 1914 the Order of the Sons of Italy, a national organization, established its New Era Lodge in Detroit. Others followed through the 1920s, and by the end of the decade there were fifteen lodges. Membership declined during the 1930s and remained small until new lodges formed in Saginaw, Kalamazoo, Grand Rapids, and Negaunee in the 1980s. The Sons of Italy continues to be active in lower Michigan. The Columbian Federation was another national organization active in Michigan in the early twentieth century.

With the development of Italian communities, people established their own churches. In 1898, after several unsuccessful starts, Father Francis Beccherini opened San Francesco Catholic church at Brewster and Rivard in Detroit, with a congregation of 1,733 Italians. The parish grew and operated a parochial school between 1911-1953.[25] Holy Family Church, located at 641 Chrysler Freeway, held its first service on 20 November 1910. The original pastor, Father John C. Vismara, a native Detroiter, was one of the first Italian Americans to record and publish the history of the Italian colony in Detroit. The third Italian Catholic church was Santa Maria (on Cardoni and Rosedale), established on 17 August 1919. Its first pastor, Rev. Joseph Ciarrocchi, was also the editor of the newspaper, *La Voce del Popolo*. The last service was held on 27 May 1983, after which the church was demolished to make way for the Chrysler Freeway. Other Catholic churches in Detroit were heavily attended by Italian parishioners and included: Patronage of St. Joseph (c. 1924, on Culver and Marcus); Church of the Madonna (c. 1925, on Oakman and Rosa Parks—formerly 12th Street); St. David's on East Outer Drive; and, Our Lady of Mt. Carmel on South Oakwood.

Italians also established Protestant churches in Detroit. The First Italian Presbyterian Mission was organized in 1914 and moved with its congregation to St. Clair Shores. Other active churches included: the Italian Baptist Church of the Savior (1912), the Italian Methodist Episcopal Church, and the Christian Congregation. Italian ministers served at the Bethel Christian Church and the Faith Christian Assembly.

While the churches flourished they functioned as the center of people's lives.[26] In the late twentieth century, as congregations moved to the suburbs the churches closed due to the lack of worshipers. Today only Holy Family Church remains at its original location and descendants of the original parishioners return for weddings and special occasions. Churches like San Francesco relocated in Clinton Township, and the First Italian Presbyterian Church became Faith Presbyterian Church in St. Clair Shores. Some of these churches maintained their ethnic identity, but other congregations assimilated into the religious mainstream.

The immigrants brought with them a rich cultural life, flourishing in artistic endeavors, theater, and music. Pasquale Palmieri, who arrived in 1858, opened an art studio. Francesco Cardoni was a sculptor from Lombardy who, prior to his death in 1901, had designed many of the monuments found in Elmwood Cemetery and in other cemeteries throughout Detroit. Venetian craftsmen and artists did much of the mosaic work found in buildings throughout the city. Vincent Aderente served as an apprentice on the "Blashfield Mural" at the Detroit Public Library.

In the field of music there were numerous success stories throughout Michigan. When opera was performed in Detroit many in the audience were from the Italian community. In the 1920s Anita Bommarito, a Detroiter and soprano, sang at fabled La Scala Opera House in Milan and also performed with the New York Metropolitan Opera. Another Detroiter, Luigi Giovannetti, sang at La Scala. Lillian Poli was the prima donna in the musical "The Chocolate Soldier."[27]

The Italian communities developed their own theatrical groups. The Teatro Italiano performed in Schiller Hall in Detroit in 1909 and the Italian Dramatic Company was also active. Italians throughout Michigan became involved in community marching bands and orchestras such as the Rome Concert Band and the Italian Colonial Band in Detroit. Throughout the twentieth century many young Italian Americans either created their own bands or joined orchestras and performed regularly on the radio.

Immigrants found it helpful, if not necessary, to assimilate into American life. In 1914 Ford investigators found that 5,000 of its 13,000 foreign employees could not speak, read, or write the English language. Officials felt that the lack of English language competency was an impediment to progress and that education was the logical answer. The company started the English School where workers learned English and American customs and financial acumen. Many Italian workers benefited from this program.[28]

Within the Italian community, people wished to Americanize their newly-arrived country folk. In 1915 non-Italians formed the National Americanization Committee to deal with assimilation. On 17 January 1921 the Italian Bureau of the Americanization Committee was established in Detroit with a legal staff that handled educational, employment, and legal problems without fees. Some three thousand men and women received instructions in citizenship classes during its first decade of operation. It also promoted the study of the Italian heritage so that children would not be alienated from their parents.[29]

The Detroit school system provided Italian Americans with the means to assimilate. Many of them entered the system unable to speak English, but quickly achieved fluency. Although many children of Italian immigrants in Detroit entered the world of work, some obtained college degrees at the University of Detroit, Wayne State University, and other institutions.

The Italian-language newspaper served as a vehicle for assimilation. It gave the literate immigrant insights and information relative to the new community, the state of Michigan, and the United States. Three Italian newspapers were published in Detroit. In May 1909, Vincenzo Giuliano published the first edition of *La Tribuna Italiana del Michigan*, which was secular and activist in outlook. Within a year the Catholic-sponsored *La Voce del Popolo* was on the streets. *L'Avvenire*, a third newspaper, concerned itself with local politics.

Over the years two of the papers continued to publish, although the Italian readership declined. In 1970 *La Tribuna* and *La Voce* merged as *La Tribuna del Popolo*. By 2000 it was called *The Italian Tribune* and continues to publish with a paid circulation of 3,500, and over 25,000 street editions available at local stores. Detroit Metro is also served by *La Gazzetta*, published in Windsor, Ontario. Cultural activities are publicized in *Curiosità*, the newsletter of the Italian Study Group of Troy.

For a number of years after 1956, the Freeworld International Academy of Dearborn published the monthly *Il Mondo Libero*. In the 1980s *The Italian American News* began its short-lived publication.[30] There is also *The Italian American*, available to members of the Italian American Cultural Center, and since November 1998, *Il Giornale* has been published in Fraser, Michigan.

Italian Americans' achievements in sports facilitated their recognition and acceptance by their peers. Many youngsters played baseball on sandlots throughout Michigan. On the major league level, in 1902, Lou Schiappacasse roamed the outfield for the Detroit Tigers. Since then several dozen Italian Americans including Rocky Colavito, Billy Martin (manager 1971-1973), and Italian-born Reno Bertoia have been part of the Tigers organization. Nick Pietrosante, Mike Lucci, and Nick Foranzo (head coach 1974-1976) appeared on the rosters of the Detroit Lions football team. Red Wings Hockey fans have cheered goals scored by Alex Delvecchio and Dino Ciccarelli. The world middleweight boxer and New Yorker, Giacobe "Jake" La Motta came to Detroit twenty-one times between 1943 and 1952 and won the world middleweight championship against Marcel Cerdan in 1949. He retained his championship belt a year later in a match against Laurent Dauthuille.

In the field of education Italian Americans continue to play an important role. Grazia Maria Cardoni Facchinetti taught Italian in 1884 to the Grosse Pointe Ladies Reading Circle and was the mother of the earliest Italian American schoolteachers. The first Italian professors in Michigan colleges and universities taught the Italian language. Today Italian Americans work as faculty, administrators, and staff in state and private colleges and universities throughout the state. Dr. John A. DiBiaggio, a Detroiter, led Michigan State University as its seventeenth president between 1985 and 1992. In recent years, Italian Americans Richard DeSantis and Al Lorenzo have served as president of Macomb Community College. Many Italian Americans have sat on the college's Board of Trustees.

Italian Americans first began to enter politics in the 1920s in the Detroit area. George A. Dondero, an attorney, held various municipal, village, township, and county offices and was elected the first mayor of Royal Oak (1921-23). Between 1933 and 1957 he held a seat in the U.S.

House of Representatives, the first Italian American to be accorded that honor. Louis Miriani, a native Detroiter, was mayor of the city between 1958-1962. Since then, innumerable Italian Americans have been elected to offices on the local and state level and have won or have been appointed to judgeships, while others have received federal positions.

Other Urban Centers in the Lower Peninsula

Pontiac, Flint, and Saginaw developed slowly during the nineteenth century, and then boomed with the coming of the automobile industry beginning in 1904. Pontiac's population grew from 14,532 to 34,273 between 1910 and 1920. General Motors entered Pontiac and purchased a number of smaller companies; many of the 254 Italians living in the city worked for the consolidated General Motors. In 1923 other Italians operated a billiard hall, tobacco and fruit stores, and candy shops. Joseph L. Marcero was the treasurer of the Pontiac Finance Corporation.[31]

Flint experienced a similar development. In 1900 Genesee County had 12 Italian residents, a total which grew to 566 thirty years later. Most of the 517 Italian immigrants who lived in Flint's south end in 1930 came from Frosinono in the province of Lazio.[32] Men owned small businesses, a few sold real estate, one worked as a pharmacist, and another ran a hotel. Women who worked outside of the home took jobs as midwives, seamstresses, candy shop keepers, and laundresses. By 1915 Italians worked for the Buick Motor Company and other auto companies. While many Italians were unskilled laborers, the auto plants hired others as machinists, grinders, electricians, engineers, and painters. Still other men found outdoor jobs as sewer contractors, bricklayers, and cement workers.[33]

In the second half of the nineteenth century, Italian immigrants went to live in Saginaw, a bustling lumbering center. By 1873, Italians worked in Saginaw as carpenters and laborers in the lumber industry. A few years later, others joined them and entered the hotel and saloon businesses. In 1884 Italians living in east Saginaw were employed primarily as laborers, musicians, and peanut vendors. During the 1890s, as in other communities, some Italians owned fruit, grocery, and candy stores. The Italian population grew from 218 people in 1910 to 420 in

Figure 5. Victor Pilot, Vittorio Santarossa, and two unknown men working on a sewer job for Mancini Construction, Detroit, 1920s. Elizabeth Pilot collection.

1930, and many of them earned their living in General Motors plants. In 1913 the Italian community was large enough to form the parish of Our Lady of Mt. Carmel. The church closed in 1992 due to the migration of its parishioners to suburbia. In 1932 the Italian Mutual Aid Society was born, operating until the late 1940s.[34]

Grand Rapids is Michigan's second largest city and is home to Dutch, Polish, and Italian immigrants. One of the earliest Italians to settle there was Caspar Campanella, a barber, who was cutting hair by 1864. As the nineteenth century unfolded the number of Italians who settled in Grand Rapids increased. Many who arrived before 1890 lived on the west side. They had migrated from Pennsylvania, where they worked in coal mines, to take jobs in the local plaster quarries.[35] Beginning in 1910 a second group of Italians moved to Grand Rapids. Soon they numbered some 500 people of whom 319 were southern Italians, primarily from Sicily and Calabria. Families also came from the cities and adjacent areas of Rome, Genoa, and Veneto.[36] By 1930 there were 742 Italians living in Grand Rapids and another 28 in other parts of Kent County.

Over the years the Italians made their living in Grand Rapids in a wide variety of ways. Machinists like Andrea Centilli worked at H. Fiebig, a carriage maker, in 1882. Five years later he took a job with William A. Kerkey Furniture. Since the furniture industry was Grand Rapids' major employer it attracted many Italians. Others found employment as fruit peddlers, who then started wholesale and retail fruit shops, groceries, and candy shops. The Grand Rapids and Indiana Railway hired Italians as laborers, blacksmiths, and carriers. Charles Gardella sold real estate. Anthony Braccio dealt in furniture, and William Guidotti made hats. Other men of Italian background worked their way into executive positions in industry.

The Italian community at Grand Rapids showed a sense of solidarity through the creation of mutual benefit societies. The Italian American Brotherhood had its own clubhouse by 1913. Of the approximately 150 Italian families in the city, roughly 110 belonged to the society. The Società Regina Margherita, a woman's society named after the queen of Italy, flourished by 1909. In 1932 the YMCA formed the Italian-American Club to promote Italian culture in Grand Rapids.[37]

The Catholic parish of Our Lady of Sorrows drew the Italian community together with greater success than other institutions. In 1889 church officials believed that there were enough Italians for a separate parish but nothing came of their concern. It was not until 1921 that Father Salvatore Cianci opened Our Lady of Sorrows church, and soon after, a school. For years the parish flourished, but declined as families moved to the suburbs.[38]

Sports, especially baseball, played an important role in the assimilation of immigrant children. In the spring of 1922 a group of Italians organized the Italian-American Athletic Club to promote sports participation among younger Italian Americans. It immediately sponsored baseball competition. As a result of this interest in sports, men such as Robert "Rocky" Parsaca and George Fulgoni became legendary in football and Tony Lomonaco won fame in boxing.[39]

By the mid-twentieth century many Italian American men and

women attained significant professional and public positions in Grand Rapids. Vincent Occhipinti became city purchasing agent after several years as assistant city clerk. Elvira Saccucci was deputy clerk of municipal court, and Mary Otterbein, née Rozzasco, headed the city's nurses division. Many other women were involved in local education.[40] Peter Secchia, a Grand Rapids businessman, served as chair of the Michigan Republican Party and ambassador to Italy during the George Bush administration (1989-1993).

Italians began to settle Muskegon in the early twentieth century. Early arrivals opened confectionery and fruit shops while others became grocers and barbers. In 1900 there were only 4 Italians in Muskegon County but in 1920 there were 259. This number dropped to 228 by the end of the decade. During this time many of the Italians found employment in the local steel foundries, brass works, furniture factories, tanneries, a tile and mosaic factory, and machine shops.[41] Within twenty years of the arrival of the first Italians in Muskegon, Father William Ducey, assistant pastor at St. Mary's church, organized the parish of Our Lady of Grace for Italian Catholics.[42]

Italians began to migrate to Kalamazoo in the early twentieth century, but by the 1920s only 104 had settled there. Many of them found employment in the local paper manufacturers in addition to the usual trades of shoemakers, barbers, confectioners, and fruit dealers. Lacking a booming automobile-related industry, however, the Italian population only reached 128 by 1930. The Italian community formed its own benevolent society, the St. Joseph Italian American Society. In 1959 the Society constructed and dedicated its own hall, and over the years they regularly celebrated the feast of St. Joseph.[43]

Michigan's capital city, Lansing, has a long history of Italian immigration. In 1886 there was an Italian peanut vendor plying his trade, and a year later John Caramella and Rosario Coscarella had opened their candy and fruit shops. The Spagnuolo family quickly followed, and started a small fruit store. By 1900 V. Muzzillo and George De Rose operated fruit stores on Washington Street and hired Italian clerks. These early Italians, who emigrated from the province of Calabria and the central town of Cosenza, wrote and told others back home of the opportunities offered by the newly emerging automobile manufacturing industry in Lansing. By 1911 recent arrivals found jobs at the Eclipse Rod Company, Seager Engine Works, and the Olds Motor Works. Soon many immigrants from the tiny village of Sant'Ippólito were living and working in Lansing.

Small Towns and Rural Areas in the Lower Peninsula

Not all of the miners and quarrymen worked in the Upper Peninsula. Rogers City is the site of large limestone deposits used in steel manufacturing. In 1910 bachelor Italians from Abruzzi began to migrate to the outskirts of Rogers City to quarry limestone. Later, families followed, residing at Calcite near the quarry. This close-knit community lasted until the Michigan Limestone & Chemical Company moved the people into Rogers City, demolishing the earlier community in 1950.[44]

Rich coal deposits beneath Bay, Shiawassee, and Saginaw counties attracted Italian miners, many of whom had first settled in the Upper Peninsula. In 1904-1905 Carlo Tarolli purchased the Six Mile Creek Mine in Shiawassee County and developed a thriving business that employed numerous immigrants. In 1907 he incorporated the New Haven Coal Mining Company and brought in Italian stockholders from Calumet. St. Charles, in Saginaw County, became the center of a flourishing Italian community. The mines continued to produce until 1952 when the last mine owned by Italians was permanently closed.[45]

Since most immigrants to Michigan came from farms, it was natural that some of them would return to agricultural pursuits when possible. Many Italians settled in rural areas in the Lower Peninsula, where the soil and climate were more conducive to farming. The first Calabrese and Sicilians to arrive in southwestern Michigan from Chicago took jobs in Benton Harbor and St. Joseph. By 1910, however, a number of them had moved to farms in Berrien County. A large-scale real estate movement in 1915 drew additional Italians from Chicago, who established berry, fruit, and vegetable farms in the vicinity of Covert, Coloma, and Riverside. In the 1920s the mobility offered by the automobile allowed some of them to develop wholesale produce businesses and a berry basket factory. By 1930 there were 450 Italians living in Berrien County. Between Holland and Grand Haven, Italians purchased farms to raise pansies, strawberries, and celery. Across the state

Figure 6. Antoni Misuraca in his winery in Paw Paw, Michigan, in the 1940s, Paw Paw Wine Company. Russell M. Magnaghi Collection.

at Monroe, the Ilgenfritz Nursery hired Sicilians because of their ability as plant grafters.

Paw Paw is birthplace of the Michigan wine industry. The oldest winery in Paw Paw is the St. Julian Wine Company. Mariano Meconi founded his Italian Wine Company in Windsor, Ontario in 1921. Thirteen days after the repeal of Prohibition, he moved his winery to Detroit. Three years later, in 1936, he relocated again, this time in Paw Paw to be closer to the grapes. Meconi changed the name of his business because of anti-Italian sentiment during World War II. St. Julian was the patron saint of his hometown in Italy. After the war, St. Julian's passed into the hands of his two sons, Eugene and Robert, and his son-in-law, Apollo (Paul) Braganini who is the father of David the current president of St. Julian. Other wine producers at Paw Paw include John Corsi who started the Frontenac Vineyards in 1937; Antonio Misuraca and G. Rouker of Detroit developed the V&J Winery in Paw Paw, also in 1937.[46]

Since the late 1960s and early 1970s the American Concord grape, which produces a sweet wine, has given way to winter-hardy, French-American hybrid grapes that can survive Michigan's harshest winters. As a result, this Italian-inspired industry is now producing fine award-winning table wines whose flourishing wineries can be found as far north as Grand Traverse and Leelanau counties.

Some Italian families in the Stevensville area of southwestern Michigan built small resorts in the 1930s to attract Chicago's Italians to relax and enjoy excellent food. The famed Tosi Restaurant is the last of these resorts still in existence. The others have given way to changing vacation tastes.

Upper Peninsula

Copper and iron deposits were discovered in the 1840s and the news quickly attracted thousands of immigrants from Europe to work in the mines.[47] In 1860 the earliest Italians—Joseph and Vitale Coppo, Joseph Gatan, Bart Quello—were mining in the Hancock area. These Piedmontese from the Canavese area arrived by way of Canada where they found Canadian, French, and Irish wives. Soon chain migration brought thousands of Piedmontese, especially from the villages of Canavese north of Turin, to the Copper Country. They found ready employment in the mines and mills of the Calumet & Hecla, Quincy, and other mining companies who desperately needed large numbers of unskilled laborers. At first the Italians shoveled ore into mine cars, but as they gained on-the-job experience and mastered the English language, some of them rose to become foremen, paymasters, and high-level supervisors in the mining echelon. The Marquette, Menominee, and Gogebic Iron Ranges were discovered in the 1840s and 1850s; the last two were developed in the 1880s. Many northern Italians migrated to these booming centers of economic activity as well.

Calumet and Iron Mountain became the two great concentrations of Italians in the Upper Peninsula. In 1910 there were some 10,000 Italians living in the Copper Country alone. Immigrant entrepreneurs ran saloons, groceries, and bakeries to cater to the growing population, while others worked as tailors, cobblers, monument carvers, toy makers, and pasta manufacturers.

The nationally known Frigo and Stella cheese brands originated in the Upper Peninsula. In the 1920s Caesar Lucchesi pioneered a bus service between South Range and Houghton, and maintained winter schedules by plowing the roads before the state of Michigan started this service.

The Italians quickly adopted the concept of the cooperative merchandising that had been initiated by the Finns in the Upper Peninsula. In towns throughout the mining country Italians opened cooperative mercantile and grocery stores between 1902 and 1917. In Iron Mountain a cooperative saloon sold beer at half of what it cost in other establishments.

Although living in a remote area, the Italians developed some sophisticated business enterprises. In 1898 a group of immigrants started the Italian Mutual Fire Insurance Company in Laurium. It remains in business in 2000 but is now known as the Great Lakes Mutual Fire Insurance Company. Upper Peninsula entrepreneurs organized the Italian Businessmen Association in 1910. This group secured the cooperation of Italian merchants, clerks, and others throughout the Copper Country by promoting moral and business interests among its members. At about the same time a group of businessmen in Laurium created the Italian Commercial Club, which encouraged economic opportunities. In 1925 the United Italian Realty Association was formed in Bessemer.

In a number of communities in the Upper Peninsula, Italians secured employment in non-mining jobs. In the late 1890s Italians enlarged the locks at Sault Ste. Marie and dug a massive power canal through the city. Upon completion, Italians found industrial employment at the Union Carbide plant, Northwestern Tannery, and Soo Woolen Mills in the city. Others crossed the Canadian border to labor in steel and paper mills, the Algoma Central Railway, and in the iron mines to the north. A number of Neapolitan railroad laborers first worked on the Soo Line in Chippewa County and later at the Cliffs-Dow charcoal-chemical plant in Marquette. At Hermansville, the IXL Lumber Company hired many Venetians to work in the lumber yards. Italians who had worked in the iron mines in the vicinity of Iron Mountain in the 1920s found jobs in the newly opened the Ford Motor Company plant, which made wooden body parts for Ford cars in neighboring Kingsford. Suddenly Italians found themselves working in an industrial auto setting.

Although the Upper Peninsula is not thought of as an agricultural region, miners and laborers developed extensive gardens and small farms for personal consumption, selling their surplus produce. In Houghton, Iron, and Dickinson counties they raised dairy cattle, hogs, horses, and potatoes. The Bono family in Calumet was one of the few to raise and sell flowers commercially.

Most Italians performed unskilled labor, but many brought radical or socialist traditions from the Old Country with them to the Upper Peninsula. Working conditions in the mines, mills, woods, and railroads left room for much improvement. Italian-sponsored organizations furthered the interests of laborers. The Workmen's Mutual Aid Society, dedicated to King Humbert I, was established in Ishpeming in 1902. In 1936 its name was changed to Workmen's Mutual Aid Society of St. Anthony of Padua. In 1914 the Workers' International Benefit Society was organized in Vulcan, in Dickinson County. These and other organizations provided laborers with sick and death benefits.

Contrary to some company histories strikes and labor unrest reverberated throughout the Upper Peninsula. In 1887 Italian railroad laborers on the Duluth, South Shore & Atlantic went on strike, and they struck again in 1894 against the Wisconsin & Michigan Railway. Italians participated in the 1894 miners' strike on the Gogebic Range and in the strike on the Marquette Range the following year. In 1904 Italians working on the excavation of the Neebish Channel in the St. Mary's River went on strike.

In 1913-1914 a major strike hit the Copper Country. The miners sought to have the radical Western Federation of Miners recognized by the mining companies, especially Calumet & Hecla. Thousands of men stayed away from their jobs for eight months. Local law officers, hired security guards, and other lawless elements repeatedly harassed the strikers. Local businessmen turned on the strikers as well.

The conservative newspaper *Il Minatore Italiano*, established in 1896, took a strong pro-company stand and soon locked horns with the union. Through the union paper, *Miners' Bulletin* (which published about one fourth of its articles in Italian), Ben Goggins, writing in Italian, challenged *Il Minatore's* position on the strike by articulating the radical perspective.

Figure 7. The Italian Fraternal Mutual Aid Society, Negaunee, Michigan, was founded in May 1890 and ended on 15 October 1962. This photograph was taken prior to 1912. The Dominic and Joyce Chiri Collection, Central Upper Peninsula and Northern Michigan University Archives.

There were a number of short-lived newspapers that promoted radical ideas and socialism among the Italian laborers. *La Demo-crazione Italiana,* published in Calumet, seems to have been a radical newspaper that lasted for only about forty-five days. *La Sentinella,* also published in Calumet put forth a radical agenda from the late 1890s until 1907. In its later years it became a socialist newspaper edited by an ardent socialist, T. Petriella.

As with most mining frontiers few Italian women arrived with the men. Many men returned to the Old Country and married wives who either returned with them or came later with their children. Women faced culture shock when they arrived in the Upper Peninsula, but most of them adjusted. They traditionally remained at home and raised their families. Many, however, kept boarders, sold wine, and produced and sold dairy products and eggs, which allowed the possibility of doubling their husband's salary. At Franklin Mine (above Hancock), Nerce Ciabitari, whose husband Angelo was a rockhouse man, had six

Figure 8. The Barasa Iron Mine (1902), located east of Negaunee, Michigan, was the only Italian-owned iron mine in the state. Russell M. Magnaghi Collection.

children. She also took care of a brother, a sister-in-law, and eleven boarders, for a total of twenty-one people in her household. Some married women and widows operated businesses, while single women worked as domestics for Italian households. In 1900 at Calumet, Margaret Gardeto and her daughter were grocers, and in Iron Mountain Sofia Baidrica and Carmela Carocci operated their own beauty salons. Throughout these communities the women organized their own social clubs, like the Italian Women's Club of Iron Mountain (1915), the Daughters of the Eternal City in Calumet (1917), or the numerous lodges of the Lady Druids. By the 1930s there was at least one women's club in each of the Italian centers of population in the Upper Peninsula.[48]

If the women had clubs, the men led the way in establishing their own mutual aid societies throughout the Upper Peninsula, beginning in 1875 with the Italian Mutual Beneficial Society at Calumet. These societies were popular, because, for a small monthly fee they provided sick, injury, and death benefits and gave the immigrant a social link to compatriots. Over the years some 130 clubs emerged and regrouped as the immigrant generation passed from the scene. Today only a few remain; the three chapters of the Paisano Clubs of the Upper Peninsula are the most active.

Religion played an important role in the lives of Upper Peninsula Italians, both Catholic and Protestant. The first Italian Catholic church in Michigan, St. Mary's, was established in 1897 in Calumet and by 1906 had some 350 active families in its membership.[49] The Italians of Iron Mountain built the church of the Immaculate Conception, which opened in 1902. During the 1890s a Waldensian missionary from Chicago ministered to Italians in Iron Mountain, while other Italian immigrants joined the local Presbyterian church. The United Presbyterian church established a mission for the Italians in Calumet in 1907.[50] The Presbyterians operated a community center for all immigrants in Caspian.

The Italian immigrants brought their love of culture with them. They published Italian newspapers and even a literary journal, *Pro Nobis*, which had a short life in Calumet. The immigrants frequently took out Italian language books from the Calumet Public Library through the 1930s. In 1928 the Italian Dramatic Group performed regularly in the Negaunee high school. In the Copper Country there was

Figure 9. First Communion at St. Mary's Church, Calumet, ca. 1911. Russell M. Magnaghi Collection.

even an Italian puppeteer who made puppets and put on perform-
ances. The Italian band became popular in local communities. In 1889
miners in Calumet formed La Banda Militare Italiana, the first such
band in the region; others quickly followed, like Vampa's Band in
Ishpeming, and the IXL Band in Hermansville.

Both Italians and the state of Michigan believed that immigrants
needed to be assimilated into the larger society in which they lived. The
state mandated that teachers be trained at institutions like Northern
State Normal School to help assimilate immigrant children. In the early
twentieth century the Italian Citizen League helped immigrants fit into
their newly adopted communities. In the small town of Ramsay on the
Gogebic Iron Range, the Italian Citizen League of Mutual Aid formed in
May 1915 to promote American citizenship among the Italian immigrants in the district, through social and political education.

Efforts at assimilation and naturalization proved successful, and
on voting day local Italians who were comparable to ward bosses in
urban areas encouraged compatriots to vote by driving them to the
polls if necessary. As soon as Italian immigrants in the Upper Peninsula
became naturalized, they became involved in local politics. As early as
April 1875, Michael Borgo served on the first Calumet village council,
and until 1906 at least one Italian served on the council. This tradition
was duplicated in many northern Michigan communities. The first
Italian immigrant to serve in the Michigan legislature was John
Deprato, a businessman from Iron Mountain. Elected on the Republican ticket in 1913, he won reelection until his retirement in 1920.
Dominic Jacobetti, a Democrat from Negaunee was the longest serving
legislator in Michigan history (1954-1994).

Throughout the Upper Peninsula, Italians and their descendants
have participated in various sports programs as players, coaches, and
spectators. In the old days bocce was played at every opportunity, and
it is still played. However most Italians Americans turned to traditional
American sports, where many excelled. A number of prominent
athletes have come from Iron Mountain. In 1915 Nino Deprato was
named All-American in football at Michigan Agricultural College. In the
1970s Steve Mariucci and Tom Izzo played football and basketball
respectively at Northern Michigan University. In 2000 Mariucci

coached the National Football League's San Francisco Forty-Niners, while Izzo coached the Michigan State University men's basketball team to the National Collegiate Athletic Association (NCAA) national championship.

Life for the Italian immigrant was not easy. America proved to be a land of opportunity but wages were low, life was radically different from what they had known, and work was the major activity of the average immigrant. Most survived the acculturation process and found solace among their countrymen in regional clubs, the Italian-language newspapers, and their families. However, others found the process too difficult. Some returned to the old country to a more familiar life, while others unfortunately turned to alcohol.

During the thirty years between 1920 and 1950 the Italian communities throughout the state responded to a number of national events. National Prohibition began in 1920 and at first the immigrants were dismayed. They quickly rallied to produce and distribute illegal alcoholic beverages throughout Michigan and the Midwest. In the Midwest, the center of distribution was at Detroit because only the Detroit River separated dry Michigan from the liquor outlets in Windsor, Ontario, a quick boat ride away.

The rise of Benito Mussolini and Fascism during the 1920s caught the attention of immigrants and non-immigrants alike. Italy was seen as a rising power on the world scene and this made many immigrants understandably proud. However, as the evils of Fascism were exposed, many Detroit Italians reacted negatively. Monsignor Joseph Ciarrocchi, pastor of Santa Maria church, joined forces with anti-Fascist labor groups in Detroit and New York City to attack Fascism. The Italian invasion of Ethiopia in 1936 further divided many Italian communities.[51]

With the outbreak of World War II, Italian non-citizen residents in the state of Michigan were faced with a dilemma. They were considered aliens of a hostile nation, Italy, and thus suspect. In 1941 18,300 Italian non-citizens lived in Detroit and eastern Michigan, the largest concentration of aliens in the state. The FBI kept them under surveillance. They were not allowed to carry or use cameras, short-wave radios, or firearms. They were under curfew. They had to carry identification papers. However, the Italian population in general was pro-America in its outlook, as evidenced in the pages of the *Italian Tribune*. Government authorities admitted that the Italian aliens were the least troublesome of classified aliens.[52] In October 1942, all restrictions were lifted for Italians classified as "enemy aliens." Despite the restrictions placed on Italian aliens, thousands of Italian Americans from Michigan served in the armed forces and many gave their lives defending the United States.

Michigan's presence in the Italian Ministry of Foreign Affairs was inaugurated in 1895 when James Lisa, a businessman in Calumet was named vice consul, as was Pietro Cardiello, a banker in Detroit in 1899. Both men were dependent on the Chicago Consulate General. Due to the growing importance of the automobile industry, a consulate was opened in Detroit in 1926. Although closed during World War II, the office was reopened in 1946, and after 1954 operated independently of the Chicago Consulate General. Today the office serves the states of Michigan, Ohio, Indiana, Kentucky, and Tennessee.

The Italian communities in Michigan have undergone change over the last half-century. Through the tenacity and hard work of the immigrants and their descendants, Italian American have progressed from unskilled laborers to some of the highest position in business, politics, law, culture, and education. Italian Americans have left the Italian urban enclaves and moved into the suburbs. Others have migrated from the Upper Peninsula in search of opportunity elsewhere. At the opening of the twenty-first century, the nearly 200,000 Italians American are ubiquitous in Michigan.

Italian Recipes from Michigan

Bagna Cauda *(Letizia Pitrone)*

Meaning literally, "hot bath," this is a traditional appetizer from Piedmont.

- 1 2-ounce can anchovies
- ¼ cup peanut or olive oil
- 1 teaspoon finely chopped garlic (more or less to taste)
- ¼ tablespoon butter
- 1 cup heavy cream

Combine anchovies, garlic (more to taste), butter and oil in a heavy bottom saucepan. Simmer very slowly for ½ hour, stirring constantly. Anchovies will disintegrate. Slowly add cream and then bring to a simmer stirring constantly (about 5 minutes).

Serve warm in a bowl or in a fondue pot in which to dip cold vegetables. Bread sticks and Italian bread are also good dipped into the *bagna cauda*. Suggested vegetables include red and green peppers, celery stalks cut into strips, savoy cabbage or romaine lettuce broken into separate leaves, or cauliflower separated into flowers. You may substitute any raw vegetables you like. Serves 6 to 8.

Bagnet *(Letizia Pitrone)*

An antipasto.

2 cups chopped parsley
1 2-ounce can flat anchovies, chopped
1 teaspoon finely chopped garlic (more or less to taste)
1 tablespoon olive oil
½ teaspoon vinegar

Combine all ingredients. Let set for a few hours to blend. Serve on crackers or sliced tomatoes.

Cheese Gnocchi *(Letizia Pitrone)*

1 pound ricotta
½ teaspoon salt
2 eggs
2½ cups flour
1 teaspoon baking powder

Combine all ingredients. This will be a dough. Roll into long strips in the shape of bread sticks. Cut into 1-inch pieces and make a print in each with the backside of a fork. Let dry at least 30 minutes. Drop into boiling salted water. When they come to the top, drain the pot. Put into a casserole with your favorite red sauce and meat, if desired.

Chestnut Soup: "Minestra di Castagne" *(Letizia Pitrone)*

Soak one pound of dry chestnuts overnight. Parboil chestnuts about ½ hour. Clean off the skins when dry.

Place chestnuts in a pan with 2 quarts of salted water. In separate pan, cook ¾ cup rice according package directions. Add cooked rice and three cups of milk to the chestnuts. Bring to a boil. If it is too thick, add more milk. This can be served hot or cold.

Asparagus Frittata *(Luigi La Marra)*

A recipe from Lazio, this frittata is traditionally made at Easter.

1 bunch of spring aparagus, cut into 1-inch pieces
¼ cup olive oil
9 eggs
salt and pepper

Place olive oil in a frying pan and sauté the asparagus until cooked. Transfer the asparagus to a separate dish and set aside. Be sure to drain any oil from the dish back into the frying pan. In a bowl, beat the eggs lightly with a fork. Warm the oil over a medium-low heat and add the egg mixture, salt, and pepper. When partially cooked, add the asparagus to the egg mixture. Cook until done and serve.

Rissoto *(Eda Vacchieri)*

Saffron risotto is a popular dish from the province of Lombardy.
Finely chop and brown an onion. Add 1-2 cups of rice and mix with chopped onions. Cook according to package directions until the rice is done.
Take chicken broth—either a can of broth or 4-5 cubes of bouillon mixed with water. Add a cube of butter. Warm the butter and then slowly pour it over the rice and broth mixture. Add Italian dried mushrooms and at least two small pinches of saffron dissolved in warm water. Cook for 20 minutes until moist and well-seasoned. Serve with Parmesan cheese.

Hunter's Delight *(Robert Bortolamoelli)*

Originally from the province of Trentino, this is a popular treat at deer camp in the Upper Peninsula.

1 bunch of parsley
garlic to taste

2 tablespoons anchovies
olive oil

Roughly chop the parsley and garlic. Add the anchovies, which can be mashed whole, or use anchovy paste, and then add olive oil until the mixture is spreadable. Serve with crackers or Italian bread.

Cardoons, the Parmesan Way *(Anna Capicchioni)*

Cardoni al parmigiano is popular in Rimini and neighboring Republic of San Marino.

3 lbs. cardoons *(cardoni)*
butter
grated Parmesan cheese
bread crumbs

The important thing is to choose the tenderest cardoons, a vegetable related to the artichoke. Clean them thoroughly and cut them into 4-inch pieces. Cook them in salted boiling water until tender; drain and allow to dry. Generously butter a baking pan. Sprinkle the pan with bread crumbs, then arrange a layer of cardoons and season with abundant bits of butter and grated Parmesan cheese. Continue layering until all the ingredients have been used. Bake at 400°F for about 30 minutes and serve immediately. Spinach, fennel, or string beans may be substituted.

Stewed Mushrooms *(Anna Capicchioni)*

Funghi in Umido are popular in Rimini in eastern Emilia.

1½ fresh field or cultivated mushrooms
4 teaspoons tomato paste
1 teaspoon basil
5 tablespoons olive oil
Salt
2 cloves garlic, crushed

Clean the mushrooms and cut into medium think slices. Heat the oil and sauté the garlic gently until it begins to brown; discard it and add the mushrooms. Whisk the tomato paste with a little hot water and add it to the pan. Season to taste with salt. Sprinkle with basil and continue cooking over a low heat for about 15 minutes, or until the mushrooms are tender. Serves 3 to 4.

Abruzzese Eggplant *(Quinto Vitale)*

This is a surprisingly unique dish. The eggplant is placed on bread and eaten in place of cold cuts.

1 eggplant
salt
hot dry pepper flakes
5 cloves garlic
1 bunch of parsley
olive oil

Peel and thinly slice the eggplant. Layer the raw eggplant in a small crock or deep bowl with a teaspoon of salt between layers. Place a small weight on the dish covering the eggplant and place in a refrigerator. Periodically drain off the water until no further water appears and the eggplant is "dry."

Clean and finely chop the parsley and garlic and mix with ½ cup of olive oil.

Remove the eggplant from the crock and place on a dish. Take the "dried" eggplant and return it to the crock or bowl layering it with the parsley and garlic mixture, and the red pepper flakes to taste. When the eggplant has filled the crock or bowl, fill the container with olive oil. Let rest for several hours. Serve on Italian bread like cold cuts.

Rose's Potatoes *(Rose Valela)*

From the Naples region.

Cut potatoes into medium slices. Finely chop the garlic and parsley. Layer potatoes with garlic and parsley, parmesan cheese, and bread crumbs in a glass baking pan. Add 1 cup of water and mix with the potatoes. Place small tabs of butter over the top. Bake at 350° for one hour.

Sicilian Cassata *(Dominic Pitrone)*

Cut a 9-inch-long, 3-inch-wide, fresh or frozen pound cake horizontally to make 3 layers.

Combine 1 pound ricotta, 3 tablespoons crème de cacao or crème de menthe, ¼ cup mini-chocolate pieces, 2 tablespoons heavy cream, ½ cup candied fruit finely chopped, and ¼ cup sugar.

Spread half of the ricotta mixture on the bottom layer pound cake. Place second layer of pound cake over the mixture and spread remaining ricotta over it. Top with the last layer of pound cake slices. Refrigerate about 2 hours or until the ricotta is firm.

Spread a chocolate frosting (see below) over the top and sides. Sprinkle with confetti cake decorations.

Chocolate Frosting

12 ounces of semi-sweet chocolate cut, chopped
¾ cup strong coffee
½ pound unsalted butter cut into ½-inch pieces

Melt over low heat until chocolate is dissolved. Remove from heat and add butter, one piece at a time. Chill until able to spread. Add 1 teaspoon of crème de cacao per cup of spreadable frosting.

Cover cake loosely and place in the refrigerator for 24 hours so that all the flavors blend.

Cinnamon Walnuts *(Agostina Giannini)*

A candied nut treat that comes from Genoa.

1 cup grandulated sugar
1 teaspoon vanilla
1 tablespoon cinnamon
2½ cups of walnut halves
5 tablespoons water

Melt sugar, cinnamon, and water over a slow fire, stirring until granules disappear. Bring to a boil and cook until the syrup threads when small amount is tested in cold water. Remove from the fire and add walnuts and vanilla. Gently stir until the walnuts are completely coated with mixture. Turn out onto a buttered cookie sheet. Break apart when cool. Each walnut will be coated with delicious cinnamon sugar.

———————————

Note: The ingredients in some of these recipes have been Americanized, but the result is the same as we remember from our childhood.

Notes

1. E. B. Osler, "Henri de Tonty," *The Dictionary of Canadian Biography,* vol. 2 (Toronto: University of Toronto Press, 1969), 633–36.
2. C. J. Russ, "Alphonse de Tonty," *The Dictionary of Canadian Biography,* vol. 2 (Toronto: University of Toronto, 1969), 631–33.
3. Vittorio Re, *Michigan's Italian Community: A Historical Perspective,* Monographs in International and Ethnic Studies 1 (Detroit: Wayne State University Office of International Exchanges, 1981), 1–3.
4. G. H. Smith, "Count Andreani: A Forgotten Traveler," *Minnesota History* 19 (March 1938): 34–42.
5. Gilbert J. Garraghan, "Samuel Charles Mazzuchelli, Dominican of the Frontier," *Mid-America* 20 (October 1938): 253–62.
6. *St. Joseph Church, Erie, Michigan, 150th Anniversary: A Historical and Biographical Review, 1819–1969* (Erie, Mich.: Privately printed, 1969), 52
7. Re, *Michigan's Italian Community,* 3–9; John C. Vismara, "Coming of the Italians to Detroit," *Michigan History* 2 (1918): 112; *Detroit Free Press,* 16 October 1853.
8. *Detroit Advertiser and Tribune,* 21 March 1859, 5 December 1874; *Detroit Free Press,* 13 June 1877.
9. Re, *Michigan's Italian Community,* 4.
10. Vismara, "Coming of the Italians to Detroit," 112–19.

11. Vismara, "Coming of the Italians to Detroit," 112–19.

12. Pietro Cardiello, "Michigan," *Bollettino dell'Emigrazione* 11 (1902): 11–12.

13. *Fifteenth Census of the United States: 1930. Population,* vol. 3, pt. 1. (Washington, D.C.: Government Printing Office, 1932), 1155. The Italian population in Wayne County was 31,572.

14. There are two stories about the origin of this name, with an equal number of advocates. One tale says that the streetcar turn-around was referred to by the immigrants as the place where the car loops or turns around, hence in broken English—*cacalupo.* The other is a literal translation—"where the wolf does his duty" or the farthest place from downtown.

15. Vismara, "Coming of the Italians to Detroit," 114–15.

16. Lois Johnson and Margaret Thomas, *Detroit's Eastern Market: A Farmers' Market Shopping and Cooking Guide* (Dexter, Mich.: Baker Johnson Book Printing & Binding, 1999), 37–42.

17. This is an inexact figure because these are only the shops identified by their obviously Italian names.

18. Vismara, "Coming of the Italians to Detroit," 115, 116–17, 119.

19. *Tribuna Italiana nel Michigan,* 1 May 1909.

20. See Ella Mae McCormick, "Detroit's Little Italy, Happy Though Crowded," *Detroit Free Press,* 12 August 1923.

21. Most of this data on lodgers can be found in the 14th Census (1920), Wayne County, Detroit, T625, reels 802 and 803.

22. *Italian Chambers of Commerce of North America: First International Convention, 28, 29, 30 September 1972* (Detroit: Privately printed, 1972).

23. *Advertiser and Tribune,* 8 June 1875; *Detroit Free Press,* 3 June 1873, 7 February 1875, 10 February 1875, 17 January 1878, 20 January 1878.

24. Russell M. Magnaghi, *Italian Clubs, Societies and Organizations in the State of Michigan, 1873–2000* (Marquette: Belle Fontaine Press, 2000).

25. "Michigan's Italian American Heritage," *Family Trails* 5 (Winter 1977–78): 7–11; Re, *Michigan's Italian Community,* 39–47.

26. Re, *Michigan's Italian Community,* 46–47; *History of the First Italian Presbyterian Church of Detroit* (Detroit: Wayne State University, 1979); *Family Trails* (1977–78): 11–12.

27. "Detroit's 5,000 Italians Plan Tribute to Pioneer's Memory." *Detroit News,* 20 June 1926.

28. "Assimilation through Education," *Ford Times* 8, no. 9 (June 1915): 407;

"Ford School Works Hard," *Ford News* 1, no. 4 (15 December 1920): 1.

29. *Detroit News,* 19 January 1931.

30. *Family Trails* (1977–78): 5–6.

31. Arthur A. Hagman, ed., *Oakland County Book of History* (Pontiac: Privately printed, 1970), 249–50; *Pontiac City Directory, 1904* (Pontiac: 1904); *Polk's Pontiac City Directory, 1922 and 1923* (Detroit: R. L. Polk, 1922 and 1923).

32. *Flint Journal,* 31 May 1988; John Iblder. "Flint: When Men Build Automobiles Who Builds Their City?" *Survey* 36 (2 September 1916): 553.

33. *Polk's Flint City Directory* (Detroit: R. L. Polk, 1915, 1919–20, 1928, 1930, 1936).

34. "Mt. Carmel Church Serves Saginaw's Italians," *Saginaw Daily News,* 23 June 1934; Saginaw city directories, 1907–1944.

35. For some time the Italian section was in an area bounded by Cherry Street, Ellsworth Avenue, and Market Avenue.

36. This group settled in the district south of Wealthy Street, west of Jefferson to Ionia Avenues, and south to Hall Street.

37. Information about these organizations can be found in the following: *Evening Press,* 18 July 1913, 3 October 1913, 11 October 1913, 13 October 1913, 1 January 1909, 29 May 1909, 20 September 1909; *Grand Rapids Press,* 29 November 1932.

38. John W. McGee, *The Catholic Church in the Grand River Valley, 1833–1950* (Grand Rapids: Privately published, 1950), 445–46; *Grand Rapids Press,* 16 May 1929.

39. *Grand Rapids Press,* 8 May 1922.

40. Z. Z. Lydens, ed., *The Story of Grand Rapids* (Grand Rapids: Kregel Publications, 1966), 555–56.

41. *Polk's Muskegon City and County Directory* (Detroit: R. L. Polk, 1908, 1921, 1936).

42. Alice Prescott Kyes, *Romance of Muskegon* (Muskegon: Privately Published, 1974), 152.

43. *Ihling Bros & Everard's Kalamazoo City and County Directory, 1902* (Kalamazoo: Privately printed, 1902); *Polk's Kalamazoo City Directory.* (Detroit: R. L. Polk, 1915 and 1926).

44. Gerald Micketti, *Little Italy in Rogers City* (Rogers City, Mich.: Privately printed, 1982).

45. Russell M. Magnaghi, *Miners, Merchants and Midwives: Michigan Upper*

Peninsula Italians (Marquette, Mich.: Belle Fontaine Press, 1987), 77–80.

46. *Kalamazoo Gazette*, 5 September 1984.
47. See Magnaghi, *Miners, Merchants and Midwives*, 77–80.
48. Ibid., 47–53.
49. Ibid., 35–38, 86.
50. *Houghton Daily Mining Gazette*, 9 July 1966
51. Philip V. Cannistrato, "Fascism and Italian-Americans In Detroit, 1933–35," *International Migration Review* 9 (Spring 1975): 33–8; *Detroit Free Press*, 19 October 1923; *Detroit News*, 1 January 1932, 11 July 1934, 22 September 1934, 10 May 1936.
52. *Detroit News*, 14 October 1942.

For Further Reference

Printed Sources

Anderson, James M., and Iva A. Smith, eds. *Ethnic Organizations in Michigan.* Vol. 1 of *The Peoples of Michigan.* Detroit: Ethnos Press, 1983.

"Assimilation through Education." *Ford Times* 8, no. 9 (June 1915): 407.

Blouin, Francis X. "'For Our Mutual Benefit': A Look at Ethnic Associations in Michigan." *Chronicle: Magazine of the Historical Society of Michigan* 15 (Summer 1979): 12–15.

Butler, James D. "Father Mazzuchelli." *Collections of the State Historical Society of Wisconsin* 14 (1898): 155–61.

Cannistraro, Philip V. "Fascism and Italian-Americans in Detroit, 1933–1935." *International Migration Review* 9 (Spring 1975): 29–40.

Cardiello, Pierto. "Michigan." *Bollettino dell'Emigrazione* 11 (1902): 10–13.

Castigliano, Attilio. "Origine, sviluppo, importanza ed avvenire delle colonie Italiane del nord Michigan e del nord Minnesota." *Bollettino dell' Emigrazione* 7 (1913): 3–22.

Copper Country Italian American Bicentennial Celebration Souvenir Booklet. Calumet, Mich.: Privately printed, 1976.

Delanglez, Jean. "The Voyages of Tonty in North America, 1678–1704." *Mid-America* 15 (1944): 255–97.

"Detroit's 5,000 Italians Plan Tribute to Pioneer's Memory." *Detroit News*, 20 June 1926.

Dictionary of Canadian Biography. Vol. 2. Toronto: University of Toronto Press, 1969, s.v. "Tonty, Alphonse," "Tonty, Henri."

Di Palma-Castiglione, G. F. "Vari centri Italiani negli stati di Indiana, Ohio, Michigan, Minnesota e Wisconsin." *Bollettino dell'Emigrazione* 6 (1915): 7–46.

Dulan, Mary Louise. *Born from Iron: Iron Mountain, Michigan 1879–1979*. Iron Mountain, Mich.: Centennial Committee, 1979.

"Ford School Works Hard," *Ford News* 1, no. 4 (15 December 1920): 1.

Garraghan, Gilbert J. "Samuel Charles Mazzuchelli, Dominican of the Frontier." *Mid-America* 20 (October 1938): 253–62.

Giglio, Joseph J. "Historical Survey of Italian Immigration in Detroit with Special Reference to the Processes Involved in the Formation of Their Spatial Patterns of Distribution." Master's thesis, Wayne State University, 1956.

Goffin, Jim. "Cheese Factory Crumbled with New Health Laws." *Daily Mining Gazette* (Houghton), 14 March 1981.

Golden Jubilee, 1913–1963: Our Lady of Mount Carmel Church. Saginaw: Privately printed, 1963.

Graff, George P. *The People of Michigan: A History and Selected Bibliography of the Race and Nationalities who Settled Our State*. State Library Occasional Paper No. 1. Lansing: Michigan Department of Education, 1970.

Guida degli Italiani del Copper Country. Laurium, Mich.: *Il Minatore Italiano*, 1910; reprinted, Iron Mountain, Mich.: The Ralph W. Secord Press, 1987.

Hyde, Charles K. *Detroit: An Industrial History Guide*. Detroit: Detroit Historical Society, 1980.

Iblder, John. "Flint: When Men Build Automobiles, Who Builds Their City?" *Survey* 36 (2 September 1916), 549–53.

Italian Chambers of Commerce of North America: First International Convention, September 28, 29, 20, 1972. [Detroit: Privately printed, 1972].

The Italian Tribune, 23 March 1984. Special issue on Italians of Detroit.

"The Italians in Detroit." *Detroit Free Press*, 12 April 1964.

Johnson, Lois, and Margaret Thomas. *Detroit's Eastern Market: A Farmers' Market Shopping and Cooking Guide*. Dexter, Mich.: Baker Johnson Book Printing & Binding, 1999.

Kavieff, Paul R. *The Purple Gang: Organized Crime in Detroit, 1910–1945.* New York: Barricade Books, 2000.

Kenny, Tim. "Roma Bakery Knows Itself." *Lansing State Journal* 30 September 1974.

Lankton, Larry. *Cradle to Grave: Life, Work and Death at the Lake Superior Copper Mines.* New York: Oxford University Press, 1991.

Love, Helen B., et al. *Global Journey in Metro Detroit: A Multicultural Guide to the Motor City.* Detroit: New Detroit, Inc., 1999.

Lydens, Z. Z. *The Story of Grand Rapids.* Grand Rapids, Mich.: Kregel Publications, 1966.

Magnaghi, Russell M. "Italians in the Upper Peninsula." In *Ethnic Groups in Michigan.* Vol. 2. *The Peoples of Michigan.* Detroit, Mich.: The Ethnos Press, 1983.

———. *Miners, Merchants, and Midwives: Michigan's Upper Peninsula Italians.* Marquette, Mich.: Belle Fontaine Press, 1987.

Mandt, Paul H. "An Old World Industry in a Modern Setting." [Frigo cheese] *National Butter and Cheese Journal* (December 1947): 1–8.

"Many Italians Once Worked in the Quincy." *Daily Mining Gazette* (Houghton), 25 August 1973.

"Many Nationalities Built Michigan." *Lansing State Journal,* 8 May 1965.

Marcoe, Reuben J. *Historical Sketch and Souvenir of Parish of St. Mary, Hermansville, Michigan (1900–1950).* Hermansville, Mich.: Privately published, 1950.

McCormick, Ella Mae. "Detroit's Little Italy, Happy Though Crowded." *Detroit Free Press,* 12 August 1923.

McGee, John W. *The Catholic Church in the Grand River Valley, 1833–1950.* Grand Rapids, Mich.: Privately printed, 1950.

Metzler, Phyllis K. "The People of Detroit: 1889." *Detroit Historical Society Bulletin* 20, no. 4 (January 1964): 4–12.

"Michigan's Italian American Heritage." *Family Trails* 5 (Winter 1977–78): 1–28.

Micketti, Gerald. *Little Italy in Rogers City.* Rogers City, Mich.: Privately printed, 1982.

Morante, Irma. "The Prociutto Connection." *Detroit Free Press* 12 November 1972.

Moroni, Giacomo. "L'Emigrazione Italiana in Florida," *Bollettino dell'Emigrazione* 1 (1913): 67–78.

Morello, Carol. "The Loyal, Spirited Italians: 'It's a Matter of Desire. . . .'" *Lansing State Journal*, 13 August 1978.

"Mt. Carmel Church Serves Saginaw's Italians." *Saginaw Daily News*, 23 June 1934.

Murphy, Edmund R. *Henry de Tonty: Fur Trader of the Mississippi*. Baltimore, Md.: The Johns Hopkins University Press, 1941.

Nelli, Humbert S. "The Italian Padrone System in the United States." *Labor History* 5 (1964): 153–67.

Niewendorp, Greg. "The Community of 'Sunny Italy' in Trimountain, Michigan." Manuscript, 1982. Central Upper Peninsula and University Archives, Northern Michigan University, Marquette.

Norman, Kathie. "The Changing Faces of the Italians in Detroit." *The Detroit Free Press*, 12 April 1964.

Noto, Scott. "Escaping "La Miseria": The Story of Grand Rapids' First Italian Residents." *Grand River Valley History* 16 (1999): 12–17.

"1853 100 Years of Religious Growth 1953," *Our Sunday Visitor*, 13 August 1953.

Pasqualini, Rita. *Comparative Study of Geographical and Occupational Mobility of Italians Active in the Construction Industry in Rome, Italy and in Detroit, Michigan*. Detroit: Wayne State University, Center for Urban Studies, 1972.

Pearsall, Margot P. "Christmas Holidays and Holy Days." *Detroit Historical Society Bulletin* 23 no. 3 (December 1966): 4–11.

Powell, Judy. *An Ethnic History of Albion*. Albion, Mich.: Privately printed, 1978.

Rankin, Lois. "Detroit Nationality Groups." *Michigan History Magazine* 23 (Spring 1939): 153–63.

Re, Vittorio. *History of the First Italian Presbyterian Church of Detroit*. Detroit, Mich.: Wayne State University, 1979.

———. "Italians [Lower Peninsula]." In *Ethnic Groups in Michigan*. Vol. 2. *The Peoples of Michigan*. Detroit, Mich.: The Ethnos Press, 1983.

———. *Michigan's Italian Community: A Historical Perspective*. Monographs in International and Ethnic Studies 1. Detroit, Mich.: Wayne State University Office of International Exchanges, 1981.

Redfern, Virginia. "Closeness—It's a Trait of Italians." *Lansing State Journal*, 9 September 1972.

Reports of the Immigration Commission. 41 vols. 61st Cong., 2d sess. Senate Doc. No. 633. Reprint (vols. 15 and 21, pt. 24), New York: Arno & *The New York Times*, 1970.

Rezek, Antoine Ivan. *History of the Diocese of Sault Ste. Marie and Marquette.* 2 vols. Chicago: M. A. Donohue & Co., 1906–1907.

St. Joseph Church, Erie, Michigan, 150th Anniversary: A Historical and Biographical Review, 1819–1969. Erie, Mich.: Privately printed, 1969.

"Small Santa Maria Parish Is 'Dying with Dignity.'" *The Detroit News,* 23 May 1973.

Smith, G. H. "Count Andreani: A Forgotten Traveler." *Minnesota History* 19 (March 1938): 34–42.

Spada, A. V. *The Italians in Canada.* Montreal: Riviera Printers and Publishers Inc., 1969.

Stark, George W. "Italian Tradition Here Began With Founding." *Detroit Free Press,* 3 November 1949.

Sturgul, Paul A. 1987. "Italians on the Gogebic Iron Range." In *Italian Immigrants in Rural and Small Town America.* Ed. Rudolph J. Vecoli. Essays from the 14th Annual Conference of the American Italian Historical Association, Staten Island, N.Y.: The American Italian Historical Association, 1987.

Thurner, Arthur W. *Calumet Copper and People: History of a Michigan Mining Community, 1864–1970.* Privately published, 1974

Vismara, John C. "Coming of the Italians to Detroit." *Michigan History* 2 (January): 110–24.

Williams, Douglas. "Wines for Sale—In Original Skin." *Detroit Free Press,* 10 October 1972.

Worth, Jean. "Hermansville." *Michigan History* 65 (March–April 1981): 17–28.

Archives and Libraries

• The Bentley Historical Library, University of Michigan, 1150 Beal Ave., Ann Arbor, MI 48109-3482; 734/764-3482; FAX 734/936-1333; *www.umich.edu/~bhl/.* Resources: interviews of Italians from throughout the state; collection includes paper materials and photographs.

• The Burton Historical Collection, Detroit Public Library, 5201 Woodward Ave., Detroit, MI 48202; 313/833-1486; *detroit.lib.mi.us/burton/index.htm.* Resources: newspaper clippings, photographs, and obituaries.

• Central Upper Peninsula and University Archives, Northern Michigan University, 1401 Presque Isle Ave., Marquette, MI 49855; 906/277-1225; *www.nmu.edu/ais/archives.htm;* e-mail: *mrobyns@nmu.edu.* Resources: oral interviews of Upper Peninsula Italians, photographs, and paper materials.

• Immigration History Research Center, University of Minnesota, 311 Andersen Library, 222 21st Ave. S., Minneapolis, MN 55455-0439; 612/625-4800; FAX 612/626-0018; e-mail: *ihrc@tc.umn.edu*; *www1.umn.edu/ihrc/*. Resources: interviews of Michigan Italians, records of the Sons of Italy, paper and photographic material.

• Iron County Historical Museum, Museum Road, P.O. Box 272, Caspian, MI 49915; 906/265-2617; *www.up.net/~iron/museums-icm.html*. Resources: clippings, photographs, paper materials, and artifacts.

• Italian American Cultural Center Library, 28111 Imperial Dr., Warren, MI 48093; 810/751-2855; FAX 810/751-3855. Resources: Italian language books, music, travel information; photographs, paper material, oral interviews, videos of local events.

• John H. Longyear Research Library, Marquette County Historical Society, 213 N. Front Street, Marquette, MI 49855; 906/226-3571. Resources: photographs, paper materials, and artifacts.

• The Library of Michigan, 717 W. Allegan St., P.O. Box 30007, Lansing, MI; 517/373-1580; *libmich.lib.mi.us*. Resources: variety of printed materials.

• Menominee Range Historical Museum, 300 E. Ludington St., Iron Mountain, MI 49801; 906/774-4276. Resources: artifacts, photographs, paper material.

• MTU Archives and Copper Country Historical Collections, J. Robert Van Pelt Library, Michigan Technological University, 1400 Townsend Dr., Houghton, MI 49931; 906/487-2505; e-mail: *copper@mtu.edu*. Resources: employee records, paper materials, and photographs focused on the Copper Country.

Sketches

The first Italian immigrant to serve in the Michigan legislature was *John Deprato*, an Iron Mountain businessman. He was first elected on the Republican ticket in 1913 and continued to win elections until his retirement in 1920.

Attorney *George A. Dondero* (1883–1968) served in various capacities in local government and as the first mayor of Royal Oak (1921–1923). Between 1933 and 1957 he was the first Italian American to represent Michigan (Oakland and western Wayne counties) in the U.S. House of Representatives. A school in Royal Oak is named in his honor.

Maria O. Giuliano (1885–1963) with her husband, Vincenzo, founded and wrote the editorials for the weekly *Italian Tribune*. After his death she took over the operation of the newspaper. She was also the co-founder with Maria Lalli of the American Italian Professional and Business Women's Club in April 1956.

Dominic Jacobetti (1920–94) from Negaunee was one of the most powerful and influential state legislators in the late twentieth century. A former miner, he served between 1954 and 1994 and was the longest serving legislator in Michigan's history. As the powerful chair of the Appropriations Committee, he was known far beyond the Upper Peninsula.

Maria Giovanetta Lalli (1905–1997) was a businesswoman who was also active in philanthropy. In 1935 she formed her own successful wine and liquor distributorship, the Universal Wine & Liquor Company. Over the years she helped create the first Italian Hour on radio station WJBK, and she promoted the Italian language at Wayne State University.

Madonna was born Madonna Louise Veronica Ciccone in Bay City, Michigan, the oldest of six children. Her parents were second generation Italian Americans with big hopes for their offspring. The loss of her mother at a young age probably gave Madonna the drive toward a successful career. After briefly attending the University of Michigan at Ann Arbor she went to New York City in 1986 and became a successful singer and actress.

Barbara Marchetti-Deschepper of Norway was the only person in the world to hold or share simultaneously the "Big Four" titles in speed skating: the National and North American Indoor and Outdoor titles, 1950–51 and 1951–52. She was also the only speed skater to win eleven major championships and tie for two others in the 1950s.

Louis C. Mariani (d. 1987), a political independent, was elected to the Detroit Common Council in 1947 and served as council president from 1950–1957. During Mayor Albert Cobo's convalescence from a severe heart attack, and again upon Cobo's death in September 1957, he was acting mayor. Mariani then won the 1957 election. As mayor he saw the completion of the Cobo Hall and Convention Arena, continued slum clearance, and supported freeway construction. In 1961, he was considered a favorite for reelection but was criticized for the city's continuing budget deficits, high unemployment, flight of people and jobs to the suburbs, and poor police relations with the black community. As a result, he lost the election to Jerome Cavanagh.

Elizabeth DeSpirt Pilot (b. 1914) only received a ninth grade education but **49** went to business school and became a successful paralegal. In recent years, in her role as archivist-historian, she has maintained a valuable personal archives on the Italians in Detroit.

From Detroit, *Sharon C. Ranucci* (1939–89) was the first woman to serve as a mediator in Wayne County and the first woman member of the Association of Defense Trial Counsel, where she served as treasurer, and former president of the Women Lawyers Association of Michigan. The University of Detroit Mercy Law School established the Sharon C. Ranucci Scholarship Fund in her honor.

Peter Secchia (b. 1937) is an Italian American businessman from Grand Rapids. He was a member of the Republican National Committee from Michigan in 1988. President George Bush named him ambassador to Italy. Secchia has established the Secchia Family Foundation at John Cabot University in Rome. Presently he is chair of Universal Forest Products, Inc.

Tony Spina (1914–1995) was one of America's most distinguished and honored photojournalists. For fifty years, Detroit-born Tony Spina photographed people and events in the news for the pages of the *Detroit Free Press*. Many of his dynamic images became news themselves.

Anne Picote de Belestre de Tonti went with Marie-Therese Guyon Cadillac to Detroit in 1702 to join their husbands, founders of the new community.

Some Italian Families in Detroit, 1701–1918

Andreoli	Cavagnaro	Forni	Muti	Raggio
Arata	Cavari	Garbarino	Oldani	Re
Arcetti	Cherubini	Gualdoni	Paganelli	Schiappacasse
Berra	Chiera	Lagorio	Paldi	Tantanella
Biotti	Colombo	Landucci	Palmieri	Tonti
Bova	Comella	Luisi	Panicali	Vecchio
Bozzalla	Cucchi	Marchese	Pannuzi	Vismara
Bozzevi	Curro	Mariano	Parozzi	Viviani
Bricchetto	De Niccola	Martelli	Pastorino	Zappelli
Bussolino	Dondero	Merlo	Pechini	
Calcaterra	Facchinetti	Moroni	Poli	

Index

Mountain, 27; Muskegon, 19;
Saginaw, 17
Ciabitari, Nerce, 25
Cianci, Salvatore, 18
Ciarrocchi, Joseph, 12, 29
Ciccarelli, Dino, 15
Cimini, George T., 10
Cipriano, Peter, 9
Clinton Township, 8, 13
Colavito, Rocky, 15
Columbian Federation, 12
Consulate in Detroit, 30
Copper Country, 22, 24
Copper strike, 24
Coppo, Joseph and Vitale, 22
Corsi, John, 21
Coscarella, Rosario, 19
Curiosità, 14

D
Daughters of the Eternal City, 26
Dearborn, Mich., 7
Degli Agli, Constantine, see Del
Halle
Del Halle, Constantine, 3
Delvecchio, Alex, 15
Deprato, John, 28, 48
Deprato, Nino, 28
De Rose, George, 19
DeSantis, Richard, 15
DeSpirt, Osvaldo, 10
Detroit, 4–16
Detroit Fruit Venders Association, 8
Detroit Lions, 15
Detroit Public Library, 13
Detroit Tigers, 15
DiBiaggio, John A., 15
DiGaetano, Nick, 11
Dondero, George A., 15, 48
Dottore, Jennie, 11
Ducey, William, 19

E
East Side, 8
Eastern Market, 8, 9
Education, 15
Ecorse, Mich., 7
Erie Township, 3
Esperti, Rose, 11

F
Facchinetti, Grazia, 15
Flint, Mich., 16
Foranzo, Nick, 15
Ford Motor Company, 6, 13, 23
Forni, Vital, 5
Franklin Mine, Mich., 25
Frigo Cheese, 22
Frontenac Vineyards, 21
Fulgoni, George, 18
Furniture industry, 18

G
Garbarino, Stefano, 5
Gardella, Charles, 18
Gardeto, Margaret, 26
Gatan, Joseph, 22
Giannini, Agostina, 37
Giovannetti, Luigi, 13
Giuliano, Maria, 11, 49
Giuliano, Vincenzo, 10, 14
Goggins, Ben, 24
Grand Rapids, Mich., 12, 17–18
Gratiot Avenue, 7
Greta Lakes Mutual Fire Insurance, 23
Grilli, Alfredo, 9
Grilli, Mary, 11
Grosse Pointe, Mich., 8
Guidotti, William, 18

H
Hamtramck, Mich., 7
Hancock, Mich., 22

Marino, Christina, 11
Mariucci, Steve, 28
Marquette, Mich., 23
Martin, Billy, 15
Mazzuchelli, Samuel, 3
Meconi, Mariano, 21
Michigan State University, 15
Miners' Bulletin, 24
Miriani, Louis, 16, 49
Misuraca, Antoni, 21
Monroe, Mich., 21
Muskegon, Mich., 19
Mussolini, Benito, 29
Mutual beneficial societies, 11
Muzzillo, V., 19

N

Negaunee, Mich., 12, 25, 26, 27, 28
New Baltimore, Mich., 8
New Era Lodge, 12
New Haven Coal Mining Company, 20
Northern Michigan University, 28

O

Occhipinti, Vincent, 19
Order of the Sons of Italy, 12
Otterbein, Mary, 19

P

Pacific, Dr. Frank C., 10
Pagano, Joseph F., 11
Paldi, Angelo, 5
Paldi, Jr., Angelo, 5
Palmieri, Pasquale, 13
Parsaca, Robert "Rocky," 18
Paw Paw, Mich., 21
Petriella, T., 25
Pietrosante, Nick, 15
Pilot, Elizabeth DeSpirt, 49–50
Pilot, Victor, 17
Pitrone, Dominic, 36

Pitrone, Letizia, 31–32
Poli, Lillian, 13
Politics, 15–16, 19, 28
Pontiac, 16
Population, 1, 16
Prohibition, 29
Pro Nobis, 27

Q

Quello, Bart, 22

R

Ramsay, Mich., 28
Ranucci, Sharon C., 50
Red Wings Hockey, 15
Republic of San Marino, 5, 9
River Rouge, Mich., 7
Rogers City, Mich., 20
Roma Cafe, 9
Rome Comcrt Band, 13
Rosetti, Louis, 10
Rouker, G., 21
Royal Oak, Mich., 15

S

Saccucci, Elvira, 19
Saginaw, Mich., 12, 16
St. Charles, Mich., 20
St. Clair Shores, Mich., 13
St. Joseph, Mich., 20
St. Joseph Italian American Society, 19
St. Julian Wine Company, 21
Santarossa, Vittorio, 17
Santelli, Toussaint, 3
Saratoni, Virginia, 11
Sault Ste. Marie, Mich., 23
Sault Ste. Marie, Ontario, 23
Schiappacasse, family, 5
Schiappacasse, Lou, 15
Schiappacasse, Luigi, 8
Secchia, Peter, 19, 50

Six Mile Creek Mine, 20
Socialists, 10
Società Regina Margherita, 18
Society of Italian Union and
    Brotherhood, 12
Sossi family, 9
Spagnuolo family, 19
Spina, Tony, 50
Stella Cheese, 22
Stevensville, Mich., 22

T
Tarolli, Carlo, 20
Teatro Italiano, 13
Tonti/Tonty, Alfonso, 2–3
Tonti/Tonty, Anne Picote, 50
Tonti/Tonty, Enrico, 2–3
Tosi Restaurant, 22
Trabbic brothers, 3
Trenton, Mich., 7
Troy, Mich., 14

U
United Italian Realty Association, 23

V
Vacchieri, Eda, 33
Valela, Rose, 36
Vampa's Band, 28
V & J Winery, 21
Venetian Jews, 5
Vismara, John C., 12
Vitale, Faro, 8
Vitale, Quinto, 35
Vulcan, Mich., 24

W
Waldensian church, 27
Warren, Mich., 8
Windsor, Ontario, 14, 21, 29
Workers' International Benefit
    Society, 24
Workmen's Mutual Aid Society, 24
World War II, 29
Wyandotte, Mich., 7